Unit

How On Earth?

Contents

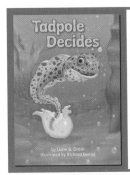

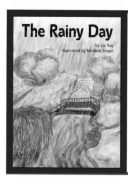

Clever Doggy

by Liane B. Onish
illustrated by Erin Mauterer

Cody and Mom were done eating breakfast. Mom noticed that the basement door was open. She said, "Cody, didn't I remind you to close the basement door last night when we got home?"

"I did remember to close it yesterday, Mom. But she opened it," Cody said.

"Where is she?" Mom asked.

There she was. Sophie, the Irish sheepdog, was sound asleep on the new sofa.

Mom said, "In order to keep the new sofa looking new, Sophie needs to sleep in the basement. She probably won't like it as well as the new sofa, but I put a cozy bed down there for her to sleep on. How did she get up here?"

"Sophie opened the door herself," Cody said.

"I don't believe it! Someone show me!" Mom said.

Sophie led the way downstairs to the basement. Mom made sure she closed the door.

"The basement has no windows," said Cody. "Maybe that is why Sophie dislikes it down here."

Sophie stood on the third step and jumped up. Her big front paws touched the doorknob and slid off. Sophie repeated the jumping and pawing until the doorknob turned.

Mom's mouth opened wide as she stood and watched. She could not believe how clever Sophie was. Mom began planning what she could do to outsmart Sophie.

After Cody returned from walking
Sophie, the basement door was open.
Tools were spread out on the floor.

"What's going on, Mom?" Cody asked.

"I'm putting in a new lock!" she
said. "I don't want to worry about
Sophie getting out of the basement
tomorrow."

"Mom, Sophie is smart. She'll find
a way to unlock it!" Cody said. And
just then Sophie let out a loud bark.

Tadpole Decides

by Liane B. Onish
illustrated by Richard Bernal

Tadpole swam beside the reeds next to Fish. Tadpole decided he was a fish.

"Hello, Fish," said Tadpole. "Look, I am a fish, too."

"Are you sure?" asked Fish with a surprised look on his face.

Tadpole said, "I have a tail like a fish. But a fish is round, and I am skinny."

Snake slithered by. Tadpole
decided he was a snake.

"Hi, Snake," said Tadpole. "Look,
I am a snake, too."

"Are you sure?" asked Snake.

"I suppose I am," Tadpole said.
"I am thin like a snake. But a
snake is long, and I am short."
Suddenly, Tadpole was unsure.

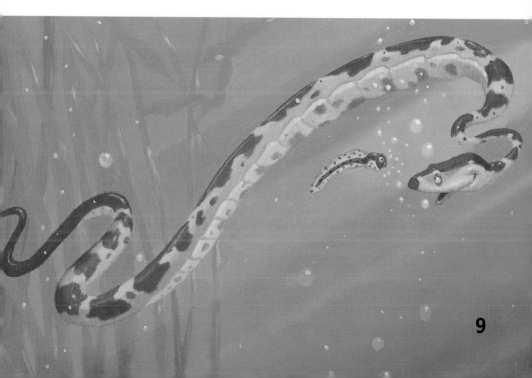

Soon, Tadpole began to change. His whole body was bigger, not skinny like Snake's. Tadpole had four legs and a tail. He was so excited!

Never in his lifetime did Tadpole think he would look like this! It felt like this was his lucky day!

Tadpole saw Turtle. Tadpole decided he was now a turtle.

"Hello, Turtle," said Tadpole. "Look, I am a turtle, too." But Tadpole did not notice that he did not have a shell on his back.

"Are you sure?" asked Turtle as she made her legs and tail go inside her large, cozy shell.

Tadpole discovered that he did not have a shell like turtle's.

"I am not sure," he said, shaking his head.

11

The next morning, Tadpole jumped out of the water.

"I am not a fish, a snake, or a turtle!" he said.

"And you are not a tadpole!" said Frog, sitting alone beside the pond.

"Look, I am a frog, too," said the grown-up tadpole. "And I am sure."

The two frogs quickly became friends and played in the sunshine.

Jamal and Rachel's
Camping Trip

by Liz Ray
illustrated by Cheryl Mendenhall

Dad took Jamal and Rachel camping in a local desert for several days.

"I don't like it here," Jamal grumbled. "It's above ninety degrees!"

"I can't see a single living thing," said Rachel. "Just rocks, pebbles, and sand blowing in the wind."

"I miss home, too," Jamal whined.

"Who's hungry besides me?" asked Dad.

Dad made a simple supper of hot dogs, pickles, and apples. They ate by the light of a lantern until there was not a morsel of food left. Then Jamal and Rachel crawled into their sleeping bags.

In the middle of the night, an odd sound filled the tent.

Rachel grabbed Dad's flashlight.
"Listen!" she said. Rachel trembled.
"I hear something. It sounds like
a howling giggle!"

"What is it?" her brother asked,
huddled in his sleeping bag.

"I think it's a coyote," said Dad.
"They live in the desert. Some
animals make their home here,
even though we haven't seen any
animals yet."

The next day, the kids and Dad went on a hike. The kids' water bottles were filled with cold water. Rachel's big hat kept the hot sun off her face.

"Look at these marks in the sand," said Dad. "I think snakes made them."

"Follow me," yelled Rachel. "Come and take a look at these mouse footprints."

17

Jamal saw a lizard scramble up
a rock. A hawk soared above them.

That night they watched the stars
sparkle like shiny nickels. One star
looked like a jewel up in the sky.
A soft wind ruffled their hair.

"I like the desert now," said Rachel.

"So do I," said Jamal. "Dad, can
we come back here next month?"

"We'll see," said Dad, humming
a little song.

The Rainy Day

by Liz Ray

illustrated by Melanie Siegel

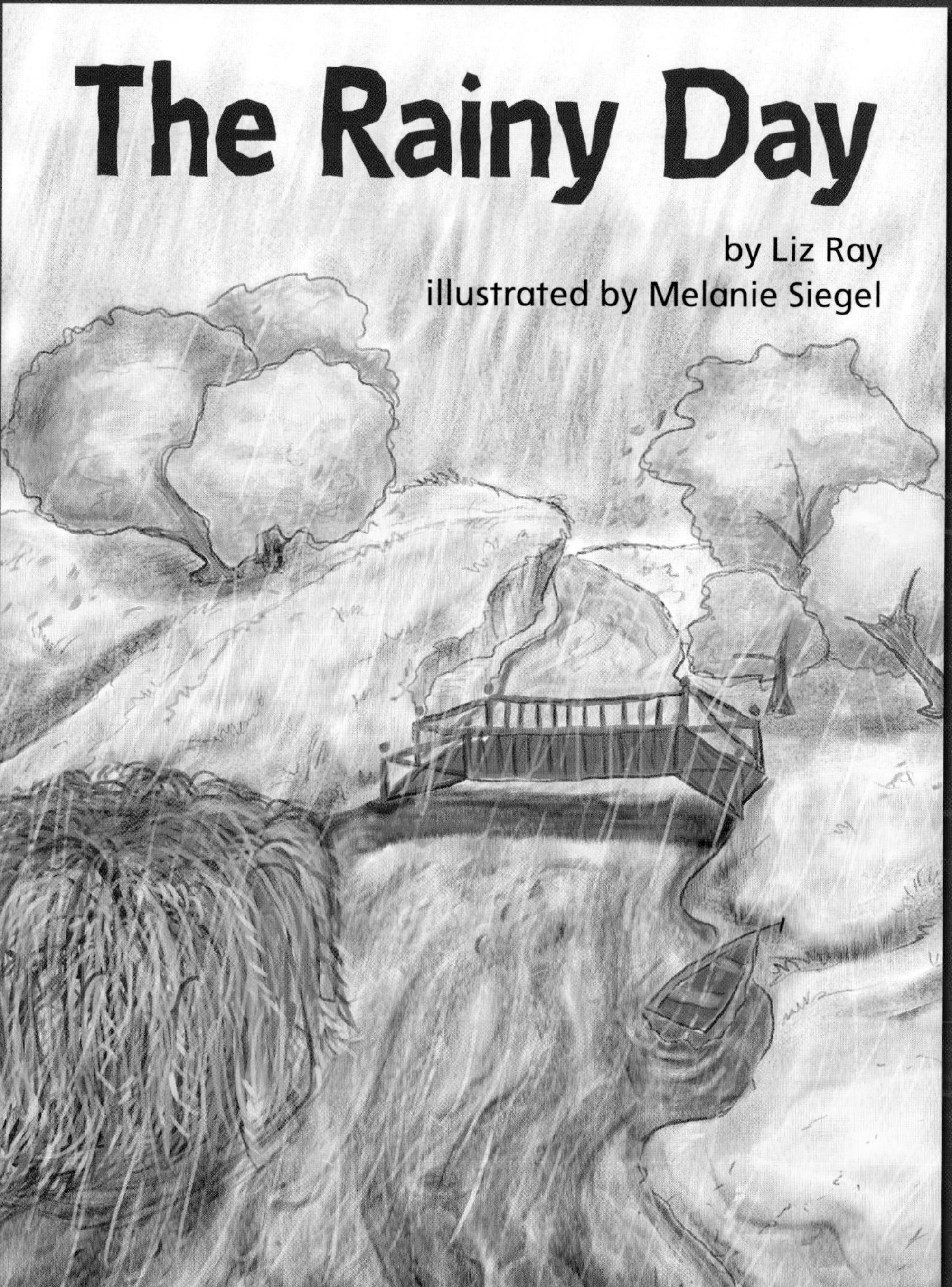

It was the biggest rainstorm
of the year. Sam had remained
inside all weekend. This was the
wettest weather he had seen in
a long time. Now Sam leaned on
his elbow and watched raindrops
slide down the window.

"I'm bored," Sam complained. "I'm
tired of reading books and playing
on the computer. Can I go outside?"

"Put on your raincoat and boots," said Mom. "And don't get near the river."

Sam felt happier now that he was able to go outside. He followed a footpath up the hill. He saw lots of footprints in the mud. A tall girl stood at the top of the hill. She looked down at the river.

"Sometimes I don't mind storms," she said. "I like to watch the rushing water."

Sam saw a stranger in a yellow raincoat standing on the footbridge. It was a man who had a house on the opposite bank of the river.

"He must measure how high the river gets," explained the girl. "We need to know if it will flood."

Sam had lots of questions about what the man was doing, but he didn't have time to ask them anymore.

As he watched the man complete his task, Sam saw a log rush downstream.

It crashed against the footbridge and knocked the man into the river. He struggled to grab a willow branch, but the water was rough and not shallow enough to stand in. The man was quickly swept into the current.

"He needs help!" yelled the girl.

Just then Sam and the girl saw a man in a rowboat. He helped the man in the yellow coat into the boat. The man was safe at last! Sam and the girl let out a loud cheer. He was glad nothing terrible had happened.

The weather forecast said it was going to be sunnier tomorrow. So Sam and his new friend made plans to go on a picnic.

How Bird Was Lured Away from Fire

by Emma Searle
illustrated by Kim Howard

Bird was an odd creature. She had wings like other birds, but she could not fly. So she walked around the towns looking for food and drink. Wherever Bird went, her feet got tired. She dreamed about flying high up in the sky and looking down at everything below.

One afternoon Bird found Fire on the ground. She hid Fire under her wing, hoping to keep it all to herself. She did not want anyone else to mistakenly find Fire.

Soon Bird grew tired and thirsty. So she went into a building to get a water bottle out of a machine.

Bird went back outside to drink her water, but she had a difficult time opening the bottle.

Just then a scientist who worked in the building stepped outside. He saw Bird struggling with her bottle. When she raised her wings, the man saw Fire.

"Bird has Fire," he thought. "Surely, that is mine! Somehow I must get it back from Bird!"

The man thought and thought about how to lure Bird away from Fire. At last he had an idea.

The man went up to Bird. "Bird, we must talk. I saw into the future last night. I dreamed you were flying!"

This upset Bird because she could not fly. But she stayed to hear more.

"You stood high on a hill with your wings completely stretched out. A gust of wind lifted you up. You were flying!" said the man. "And there was no wire! You didn't have any trouble flying at all."

Bird pretended not to care about the dream. But the next day, she stood on a hill. She put Fire on the ground. Then she stretched out her wings, looked ahead, and waited. Just then the man snatched Fire and ran away.

The man was happy again. Now he could use Fire to help people of all cultures. He knew he could travel throughout the land and show them how to use Fire in many safe ways.

Unit 6: How On Earth?

to use with *Why Fir Tree Keeps His Leaves* **WORD COUNT: 291**

DECODABLE WORDS

Target Phonics Elements

Closed Syllables:

after, clever, doggy, getting, jumped, jumping, little, planning, until, windows

Open Syllables:

asleep, began, Cody, cozy, going, Irish, open, opened, remember, remind, sofa, Sophie, repeated, returned

HIGH-FREQUENCY WORDS

door, front, order, probably, remember, someone, tomorrow, what's, worry, yesterday

Review: about, do, done, from, of, one, said, sure, to, want, was, were, what, you

STORY WORDS

believe, floor, noticed

31

to use with *Pedal Power* **WORD COUNT: 334**

DECODABLE WORDS

Target Phonics Elements

CVCe Syllables:

became, beside, face, hopeless, inside, lifetime, like, made, Snake, Snake's, sunshine, Tadpole, whole

HIGH-FREQUENCY WORDS

alone, became, beside, four, hello, large, notice, round, suppose, surprised

Review: are, away, friend, have, of, said, sure, to, was, you

STORY WORDS

body, imagined, minute, two

to use with *Dive Teams*

WORD COUNT: 288

DECODABLE WORDS

Target Phonics Elements

Consonant + le (el, al) Syllables:

animals, bottles, grumbled, huddled, jewel, little, local, middle, morsel, nickel, ruffled, scramble, several, simple, single, sparkle, trembled

HIGH-FREQUENCY WORDS

above, brother, follow, listen, month, soft, something, song, who's, wind

Review: again, any, are, come, do, have, haven't, live, living, of, one, said, some, their, though, to, was, water, were, what

STORY WORDS

coyote, desert

to use with *The Life of a Dollar Bill*   **WORD COUNT: 327**

DECODABLE WORDS

Target Phonics Elements

Vowel Team Syllables

boat, books, boots, coat, complained, day, down, downstream, elbows, enough, explained, flood, followed, footbridge, footpath, footprints, high, house, know, leaned, looked, loud, measure, need, needs, out, outside, playing, rain, raincoat, raindrops, rainstorm, rainy, reading, remained, rough, rowboat, saw, shallow, seen, stood, tall, weather, weekend, willow, window, yellow

HIGH-FREQUENCY WORDS

against, anymore, complete, enough, river, rough, sometimes, stranger, terrible, window

Review: about, into, nothing, of, said, to, tomorrow, was, water, who, your

STORY WORDS

computer, current, opposite, questions

to use with *Poetry: A Box of Crayons; What Story is This?* **WORD COUNT: 368**

DECODABLE WORDS

Target Phonics Elements

r-Controlled Syllables

Bird, birds, care, creature, cultures, Fire, future, hear, her, herself, lure, luring, more, surely, tired, there, thirsty, under, water, wire

HIGH-FREQUENCY WORDS

afternoon, ahead, anyone, everything, pretended, scientist, somehow, throughout, trouble, wherever

Review: about, again, any, around, away, because, building, else, from, have, idea, into, many, of, one, other, people, said, to, want, was, who, were, you, your

STORY WORDS

machine, difficult

35

HIGH-FREQUENCY WORDS TAUGHT TO DATE

Grade K

a	been	jump	straight	anything	even	know
and	before	knew	sure	apart	every	laugh
are	begin	know	their	are	everybody	learn
can	below	laugh	then	around	everyone	leaves
do	better	learn	there	away	eyes	light
for	blue	live	they	baby	fall	like
go	boy	love	thought	ball	family	little
has	brought	make	three	beautiful	far	live
have	build	many	through	because	father	long
he	buy	minutes	today	been	few	look
here	by	more	together	before	field	love
I	call	mother	too	began	find	many
is	carry	move	two	begin	first	maybe
like	certain	never	under	behind	five	me
little	change	new	until	below	found	meant
look	climbed	no	up	better	from	minutes
me	come	not	upon	bird	flower	morning
my	could	nothing	use	blue	food	more
play	does	now	very	body	for	mother
said	done	of	walked	both	friends	move
see	down	old	want	bought	funny	my
she	early	once	warm	boy	girl	myself
the	eat	one	water	brought	give	neither
this	eight	only	way	build	go	never
to	enough	open	were	building	goes	new
was	every	or	who	busy	good	nothing
we	eyes	orange	why	buy	gone	now
what	fall	other	work	by	great	number
where	father	our	would	carry	group	o'clock
with	find	out	write	certain	grow	of
you	four	over	yellow	change	happened	off
	friends	people	your	cheer	happy	often
Grade 1	from	place		children	has	old
about	full	poor	**Grade 2**	city	have	on
across	funny	pretty	about	climbed	he	once
after	girl	pull	after	cold	head	one
again	give	put	again	colors	hear	only
against	goes	ride	ago	come	heard	open
air	gone	run	air	could	heavy	or
all	good	saw	along	country	help	orange
along	great	says	all	didn't	here	other
also	grew	school	almost	do	house	our
always	head	searching	also	done	how	out
another	help	should	always	don't	hundred	outside
any	her	shout	America	down	hurt	over
around	house	show	among	draw	idea	own
away	how	so	and	during	I'll	paper
ball	instead	some	animal	early	inside	part
be	into	soon	another	eat	instead	people
because	it	sound	any	eight	into	person
			answer	either	isn't	picture
				else	knew	places
				ever		play

36

please	school	sorry	these	try	wash	words
pretty	searching	sounds	they	turned	watch	work
problem	second	special	this	two	water	world
pull	see	start	those	under	were	would
pushed	seven	started	though	understands	what	year
put	several	stood	thought	until	where	yellow
questions	she	story	three	upon	which	yes
read	should	straight	through	touch	who	you
ready	show	strong	to	very	whole	young
right	sky	sure	today	voice	why	your
said	sleep	talk	together	walk	without	
Saturday	small	the	too	want	woman	
saw	some	their	took	warm	won	
says	soon	there	toward	was	won't	

DECODING SKILLS TAUGHT TO DATE

CVC letter patterns; short *a*; consonants *b, c, ck, f, g, h, k, l, m, n, p, r, s, t, v;* inflectional ending *-s* (plurals, verbs); short *i*; consonants *d, j, qu, w, x, y, z;* double final consonants; *l* blends; possessives with *'s;* end blends; short *o;* inflectional ending *-ed;* short *e;* contractions with *n't;* *s* blends; *r* blends; inflectional ending *-ing;* short *u;* contractions with *'s;* digraphs *sh, th, ng;* compound words; long *a (a_e),* inflectional ending *-ed* (drop final e); long *i (i_e);* soft *c, g, -dge;* digraphs *ch, -tch, wh-, ph;* inflectional ending *-es* (no change to base word); long *e (e_e),* long *o* *(o_e),* long *u (u_e);* silent letters *gn, kn, wr;* 3-letter blends *scr-, spl-, spr-, str-;* inflectional endings *-ed, -ing* (double final consonant); long *a (ai, ay);* inflectional endings *-er, -est;* long *e (e, ea, ee, ie);* *e* at the end of long *e* words; long *o (o, oa, oe, ow);* 2-syllable words; long *i (i, ie, igh, y);* 2-syllable inflectional endings (changing *y* to *ie*); long *e (ey, y);* inflectional ending *-ed* (verbs; change *y* to *i*); *r*-controlled vowel /ûr/*er, ir, ur;* inflectional endings *-er, -est* (drop final e); *r*-controlled vowel /är/ *ar;* abbreviations Mr., Mrs., Dr.; *r*-controlled vowel /ôr/*or, oar, ore; ea* as short *e;* diphthong /ou/ *ou, ow;* final *e* (mouse, house); diphthong /oi/*oi, oy;* prefixes *re-, un-;* variant vowels /ù /*oo,* /ü/*oo, ew, ue, u_e, ou;* possessives; variant vowel /ô/*a, au, aw, augh;* singular and plural possessive pronouns; 2-syllable words; *r*-controlled vowel /âr/*air, are, ear;* contractions; open syllables; closed syllables; final stable syllables; vowel digraph syllables; *r*-controlled vowel syllables; vowel diphthong syllables; short *a, e, i, o, u;* consonant blends *dr, sl, sk, sp, st;* consonant digraphs *ch,-tch, sh, th, wh, ph;* long *a (a_e), i (i_e), o (o_e), u (u_e);* soft *c* and *g;* long *a (a, ai, ay, ea, ei);* consonant blends *scr, spr, str;* long *e (e, ea, ee, ey, ie, y);* prefixes *re-, un-, dis-;* long *i (i, ie, igh, y);* compound words; long *o (o, oa, oe, ow);* inflectional endings *-s, -es;* long *u (ew, u, ue, u_e);* inflectional ending *-ing,* *r*-controlled vowels *er, ir, ur, ear, eer, ere, ar, or, oar, ore, air, are;* inflectional endings *-er, est;* silent letters *gn, kn, wr, mb;* inflectional ending *-ed;* suffixes *-er, -est;* prefixes *re-, un-, dis-;* diphthong *ou, ow;* diphthong *oi, oy;* variant vowel *oo, ui, ew, ue, u, ou, oe;* variant vowel *oo, ou;* variant vowel *au, aw, a;* suffixes *-ful, -less;* inflectional ending *-ed;* closed syllables, open syllables, consonant + *le* syllables; vowel-team-syllables; final *e* syllables; *r*-controlled vowel syllables